# Radical Productivity

Master Your Time, Eliminate Procrastination, and
Radically Improve Your Productivity

By M Salek

Copyright © 2019 by M Salek

All rights reserved. This book or any portion thereof may not be reproduced or used in any manner whatsoever without the express written permission of the publisher except for the use of brief quotations in a book review.

No part of this book may be reproduced, stored in a retrieval system, or transmitted in any form or by any means, electronic, mechanical, photocopying, recording, scanning, or otherwise, without the prior written permission of the publisher.

First edition - Aug 2019

Disclaimer

All the material contained in this book is provided for educational and informational purposes only. The author, his agents, heirs, and assignees do not accept any responsibilities for any liabilities, actual or alleged, resulting from the use of this information. No responsibility can be taken for any results or outcomes resulting from the use of this material.

This book is not "professional advice." The author encourages the reader to seek advice from a professional where any reasonably prudent person would do so.

While every attempt has been made to provide information that is both accurate and effective, the author and his affiliates cannot assume any responsibility for errors, inaccuracies or omissions, including omissions in transmission or reproduction. Any references to people, events, organisations, or business entities are for educational and illustrative purposes only, and no intent to falsely characterise, recommend, disparage, or injure is intended or should be so construed.

Any results stated or implied are consistent with general results, but this means results can and will vary. The author, his agents, and assigns, make no promises or guarantees, stated or implied. Individual results will vary and this work is supplied strictly on an "at your own risk" basis.

# Table of Contents

| | |
|---|---|
| What Will You Learn | 5 |
| The Problem With Productivity (and The Costs) | 6 |
| The Greatest Myth about Productivity | 11 |
| True Productivity = ? | 14 |
| The Myth about Early Risers | 18 |
| The Myth about Multitasking | 23 |
| How To Start Your Day Right | 27 |
| How 20 Minutes Can Transform Your Productivity | 34 |
| Planning Your Time Effectively | 44 |
| Planning For Impact | 49 |
| How To Be Productive Even When You're Lazy | 59 |
| Dealing With Procrastination: The Five-Minute Technique | 64 |
| Focusing On The Long Term, One Step At A Time | 69 |
| How To Keep Getting Better | 75 |
| Taking Care Of The Short Term | 79 |
| Recap | 84 |
| Next Steps | 87 |
| Closing Thoughts | 90 |
| About The Author | 94 |
| References | 95 |

# What Will You Learn

Here are a few things you will learn in this book (or... why you really need to read this book):

1. The biggest problems with productivity right now
2. Why being an early riser is not always a good idea, and does not work for everyone (and what to do instead)
3. How to start your day to have the most impact
4. How to effectively deal with emails
5. Step by step guide for creating an effective morning system
6. Five ways to effectively take breaks (breaks that will help you)
7. What not to do when taking a break
8. How to finally get a handle on your time
9. Elon Musk's productivity hack
10. What you can learn from Eisenhower about time management
11. How to deal with procrastination (two effective strategies that will help you eliminate productivity)
12. How to be productive even when you are procrastinating
13. How to keep getting better
14. How to make the most of your present moment
15. How to do work that matters, and has impact

Let's begin.

# Introduction

## The Problem With Productivity (and The Costs)

Productivity is a big issue, and for good reason. Being productive not just benefits us individually; it also makes a big difference from a collective societal point of view.

Lack of productivity is costly - for both businesses and for us personally. As a 2016 report from the US Bureau of Labor[1] found, productivity levels are going down across the board - this is not good news for businesses. It gets worse - according to the APA, roughly $500 billion is lost every year[2] because of workplace stress, a big cause of which is a lack of productivity and effectiveness.

Lack of productivity also takes a major toll on our individual health and well-being. This is, in fact, one of the biggest causes of workplace stress - one that comes at a big cost, as mentioned earlier.

Then there are the other costs that lack of productivity results in, including job dissatisfaction, depression, lack of income, unhappiness, stress, anxiety, mental health problems, etc. But that's not the worst - author Jeffrey Pfeffer, a business theorist, explained in his book "Dying for a Paycheck" how stress and overwork result in about 120,000 preventable deaths every year in the US. Stress and overwork that true productivity can minimise, if not get rid of.

Suffice to say, being unproductive is costly.

### Why did I write this book

Productivity is a topic I have been interested in for as long as I can remember. To be honest, it was more of an obsession than just an interest. Productivity is a passion for me - I am always looking for better ways of doing things, of being more productive, of making more impact with my time. I have spent thousands of hours learning about it, and trying out what I learned. All that time and energy that I spent has been useful - it has transformed my productivity, and those of the people I have worked with.

This is not my first book or even my second. Writing about productivity has been on my list of books to write for a while (ever since I first considered writing a book). When I was considering the topics for my third book, I thought about writing a book about personal growth, or peak performance. Productivity was actually my third option. But this book is the one that resonated with me the most. It was time. And here it is.

### How can this book help you

I have picked up a few things over the 16+ years that I spent on learning how I can be more effective. I have made lots of mistakes; I found what works and what doesn't, I figured out better ways of doing things, and I continue to learn. This book is the fruit/amalgam of all those years of learning, and trials and errors.

I wanted to create a book, a manual if you will, that has the potential to massively impact people's productivity, and I believe I have done so. But there is only one way to really find out, and that's for you to learn the lessons in this book, and then apply them.

Note: Throughout this book, I have often used "effectiveness", "true productivity" and "radical productivity" synonymously. The context will make that clear.

With that bit of housekeeping out of the day, let's get you started on your journey of radical productivity.

### Keep your mind open

Before you get started, I want you to understand something - you need to keep your mind open. If you go through this book with a closed mind, it will be very challenging to benefit from what you learn. Here is a story to illustrate my point:

Once upon a time, a university lecturer visited a Zen master to learn about Zen. He asked the Zen master to teach him the meaning of Zen. The Zen master, in response, quietly poured a cup of tea.

The cup filled up, but he did not stop.

He continued to pour even after the cup overflowed.

The lecturer grew impatient and asked the Zen master why he kept pouring tea even after the cup was full. The Zen master told the lecturer that he was attempting to understand Zen when his mind was already full of preconceptions. That if he continued in that state, the teachings about Zen would simply overflow and not stick, just like it did for the tea.

Once the cup was full, pouring more tea did not help - all it did was create a mess. The point the Zen master illustrated was this - if you already have preconceived notions about something (and have a closed mind), it will be difficult (if not impossible) to accept new knowledge.

The new understanding can only stick when your mind is open. Similarly, it is important to keep your mind open to make the most of what you learn in this book because there will be concepts that will challenge your existing understanding of productivity. Some things may even seem counterintuitive.

But they work.

That said, they can only work for you if you apply them, and that can't happen if you refuse to accept what does not fit your existing model of productivity.

Don't knock them until you've tried them.

**Onward...**

Time is our most valuable resource, and it is limited. Not being productive means you waste time that you will never get back. Most people live their lives without a care for how they spend their time, only to regret it later.

Do not be one of those people.

You cannot afford to be one of those people if you want your work to have impact - and your life to have meaning.

Life is short, so you need to make the most of the limited time you have. Just keeping busy isn't enough if you want to be effective, and want your work to matter.

That said, life is not about wringing every bit of time and energy you can to work. Life is about impact.

The two points might seem contrary, but they are not. Time is a limited resource and you can't afford to waste it, but that does not mean you should be working all the time. Balance is key, and impact is what is important.

Bottom line, life isn't about working every waking hour of your day. It is about having the most impact with your time (and energy) so that you can enjoy your life without being a slave to your work.

And what you learn in this book will put you on a solid footing to do just that.

Moreover, if "not having enough time" is a common worry for you, the principles and strategies in the following chapters will help you get a firm handle on your time, and much, much more.

Let's get started.

*Never mistake motion for action* - Mark Twain

# Chapter 1

## The Greatest Myth about Productivity

Would you like to know what the greatest myth about productivity is (and how it's holding you back)?

Here it is - that to be productive you need to do as much as possible, and more.

And by that mandate, if you are not doing a LOT of things, you are not really productive.

That's the common perception of productivity.

And it is absolutely, positively, and entirely...

False.

This is the biggest myth about productivity that has ever existed.

The lie that is behind the current belief of worthlessness that people feel when they have not done a hundred different things in a day.

The myth that causes a lot of stress, anxiety, and feelings of ineptitude. So why is this belief about productivity false?
Because at the end of the day, it all comes down to impact.

If what you do has no impact, it makes no difference how many things you do or how many hours you have spent on it. If there is nothing to show for despite slaving away for many hours and doing numerous things, then what exactly did you accomplish? What was the point?

And that is unfortunately what this myth about productivity perpetuate.

To be productive, and I mean really truly productive, you need to radically alter your perception of productivity. You need to not just think differently, you need to completely flip it over. You need to completely rethink your beliefs about productivity.

Because productivity is NOT just about how many things you do. With me so far?

Great, then you are ready to discover what true productivity is really about, which is where the next chapter comes in.

*Improved productivity means less human sweat, not more - Henry Ford*

# Chapter 2

## True Productivity = ?

So in the last chapter, you learned about the biggest productivity myth.

And it is a dangerous myth, one that causes a lot more harm than good. In the long term it really doesn't add up, what with the toll it takes on health, well-being, happiness, and more. That myth about productivity is one of the biggest reasons why people have extremely poor work-life balance, why a lot of people feel shitty even after putting in huge amounts of time and effort into their work, and why so many people feel stressed.

This is a myth that needs to be obliterated.

We need to stop thinking about productivity in terms of doing as much as we possibly can. One study[1] even found that reducing the number of hours worked can have a positive impact on a person's productivity. This goes on to show how squeezing every available second of your day for work is not what leads to true productivity.

But you might be wondering by this stage - so if true productivity is not about doing as much as possible, if it is not about filling your days with lots and lots of things to do, then what is it about?

And here is the answer to that... effectiveness.

You are effective when your work has impact, when it makes a difference, when you have something to show for the time and energy you have put into your work.

So **true productivity = effectiveness**

Effectiveness is all about impact - as I mentioned earlier, you can slave away for hours and days and weeks, months, even years, but if your work doesn't really make any impact the activities become pointless.

Let me give you an example: imagine spending several hours every day promoting your business on social media, posting multiple times, interacting with people, liking, sharing, commenting and so on. You do this for months. But all of that activity and time spent then leads to nothing and does not benefit your business in any way. So what was the point? And more importantly, would you consider that time and energy you spent as being productive?

This is a very real example by the way - I have come across several entrepreneurs who did just this. But this is not a place to talk about social media's effectiveness or the importance of it or its benefits. If you want to learn about social media, I suggest consulting someone who knows what s/he is doing.

This is what I want you to understand - just because you are doing things does not make you productive.

Activity ≠ Productivity

So I am going to redefine productivity.

**Time + Impactful work = Productivity**

Productivity is NOT about doing as many things as you can. It is about doing work that counts.

It's about having impact with your work. This was demonstrated in a famous research[2] by Psychologist Anders Ericsson, which found that the best performers were not the ones who spent the most time practising, but rather the ones who most productively made use of their time.

The importance of quality over quantity was further demonstrated in a 2015 study published in The Economic Journal[3]. The study found that long working hours usually leads to lower productivity, not higher. But not just that, according to yet another research[4] long working hours were also found to have an adverse impact on our health.

Clearly working long hours isn't the answer to being truly productive.

If you want to be truly productive, you need to stop thinking about doing as much as you possibly can and spending every waking hour doing things. Instead, you need to start focusing on the quality of the work you do. This is because the quality of the work you do matters FAR more than the quantity of the work you do.

Productivity, and I mean true productivity, is NOT about quantity.

It is about quality.

Once you have truly understood this concept (quantity, not quality), you are well on your way to transforming your productivity. In fact, if this is the only thing you learn from this book, you will still be way more productive than most people.

That said, this is just the beginning. Your journey to radically improve your productivity is only getting started. The rest of the chapters in this book will alter a few more perceptions, disprove a few more myths, and teach you strategies that will radically transform your productivity.

Ready?

Great. Onto to the next chapter.

When you embrace your difference, your DNA, your look or heritage or religion or your unusual name, that's when you start to shine - Bethenny Frankel

# Chapter 3

## The Myth about Early Risers

So far you have learned about the greatest myth about productivity, and what true productivity is.

In this chapter, I am going to debunk another big productivity myth: that you need to be an early riser to be productive.

This myth has been around for nearly as long as... well, it's been around forever.

And common sense would dictate that it makes sense - after all, the earlier you start, the more hours you get.

In theory, that is correct.

But it is not correct in practice.

There are two major, fundamental flaws with this concept:

1. It encourages people to work as much as possible (the whole quantity fallacy), which can and often does result in a sacrifice of proper sleep. Terrible idea.

2. Now for the second major flaw with the early riser concept - it assumes that everyone's bio-physiology works in exactly the same way. That everyone's Chronotype is the same - completely inaccurate.

Let's look at these flaws more closely.

**Sleep**

It's common knowledge just how important a good amount of sleep is for you (minimum 7-9 hours, according to the Sleep Foundation[1]). Sacrificing your sleep for work may work in the short term, but it plays havoc with your health in the long term. Trust me, I know. I've been there, done that.

In my early twenties, I often slept only 2 hours a night - sleep seemed like a waste. I did that for several years. Do you want to know what happened around my late-twenties?

My health was in a terrible state. I looked like a skeleton. My energy level was completely shot. Often I couldn't stay awake past 6 pm!

It was not pleasant, to say the least. So learn from my mistakes, and do not sacrifice your sleep for work. Make sure to get at least 7-9 hours of sleep every day.

Exhaustion detrimentally affects our ability to make decisions, yet another reason why a lack of sleep does more bad than good. But there's more - a study published in the journal Sleep[2] found that early morning work usually results in insufficient sleep and increased levels of stress and anxiety, which ultimately results in a lack of productivity. This is not the first time researchers found a correlation between early rising and lack of productivity - an earlier French study[3], published in July 1987, found similar indications.

Sleep is also essential for replenishing the limited mental energy we all have. A 2014 study published in the journal Motivation Science[4] found that the amount of mental energy we have is not unlimited. Ever felt completely drained after a challenging day, a day that involved lots of problem-solving and decisions? That is because you depleted your mental energy, and maybe then some. The best way to fill up your mental energy reserve is to sleep. Guess what happens when you have a mentally exhausting day, and then don't get enough sleep...

If you still need convincing that lack of sleep is bad for you (and for your work), here's an interesting stat for you: tired employees cost American businesses $63 billion in lost productivity a year[5].

Turns out, "early to rise" isn't the productivity golden rule it has been made out to be.

**Chronotype**

The age-old assumption that everyone is (or should be) an early riser is a flawed concept. Nothing could be further from the truth. With developments in medicine and health sciences, we are starting to better understand just how different each of our internal mechanism is. There is a reason why personalised medicine is one of the fastest-growing fields in medicine right now (with estimated global market size of USD 1.57 trillion in 2018[6]).

So personalisation is important, and this applies to our sleep pattern too.

Enter: Chronotype.

Our chronotype is our body's biological clock. It is what ultimately determines the ideal time for us to sleep. This is not conjecture, or an arbitrary decision made by someone on a whim, but is based on our genes - the PER3 Gene, to be specific[7]. Not everyone's chronotype is the same, so it should hardly come as a surprise that one standard time for going to sleep or waking is not optimal for everyone. This is why morning people struggle to work late, and why night owls struggle to wake up early. If you have ever experienced one of these scenarios, this is the reason why.

Morning person or night owls are not the only chronotypes, however. According to Dr. Michael Breus (author of "The Power of When" and one of the leading authorities on chronotype), there are four main chronotypes: lions, dolphins, wolves, and bears. If you chronotype), there are four main chronotypes: lions, dolphins, wolves, and bears. If you want to find out more about your chronotype, Dr. Breaus has a quiz that you can check out at thepowerofwhenquiz.com.

The point is this - being an early riser does NOT work for everyone. So if you are one of those people for whom getting up early is a struggle, stop beating yourself up over it.

The same goes for all of you out there who struggle to stay up late.

As it turns out (thanks to the advancements in modern science), early to bed and early to rise does actually NOT make a person healthy, wealthy and wise...

So work with your chronotype, not against it. If you are naturally an early riser, wake up early. If you are not, however, then stop forcing yourself to wake up early. Choose a schedule that works with your chronotype. That way you will give yourself a massive boost when it comes to your effectiveness.

Now, working in accordance with your Chronotype might involve changing your working hours, which means looking into flexible working. But that's not a bad thing.

If you run your own business, introducing flexible working hours that will take advantage of your team members' individual chronotype means you will get them at their best time. This applies to you even if you work for someone. As research has shown[8], flexible working does not have any adverse impact on productivity - so if changing your work schedule fits your chronotype better, it is definitely worth looking into.

**Moving forward**

Rather than forcing yourself to wake up early and then suffering, as a result, opt for waking up when it feels natural.

And above all, don't forget to get a good amount of sleep.

Proper sleep and working to a schedule that augments your chronotype will give your productivity a massive boost. These two factors alone can completely transform your ability to be truly productive.

—

You are on a roll, but don't stop here, because in the next chapter you will learn how to start your day strong so that you can really make the most of your day and further improve your productivity (and results).

*To do two things at once is to do neither -*
*Publius Syrus*

# Chapter 4

## The Myth about Multitasking

In the last few chapters, we reviewed and debunked two of the biggest myths surrounding productivity - myths that in the end cause more a lot more harm than good.

But that was not the end. In this chapter, we will examine yet another big myth about productivity.

That to be really productive, you need to be good at multitasking. Spoiler alert: That is absolutely not true.

**Multitasking is not productive?**

Multitasking has long been considered one of the key characteristics of those who are productive. Here is the fundamental idea behind that idea - the more you can do at the same time, the more you can get done.

Sounds about right doesn't it? After all, if you can do two things at a time, then surely you will be more productive than someone who only does one thing at a time?

Here is where it falls down - our brains are not just not designed to do more than one thing at a time[1].

When we do several things at a time, it leads to:

- a decrease in our ability to focus. You can never achieve the flow state if you are multitasking.

- a fall in the quality of our work. The more distracted you are, the less attention you end up paying to the work at hand, which impacts the quality of your work. In that sense, multitasking is inversely proportional to effectiveness - the more things you do at a time, the less effective you will be, and vice versa.

- increased levels of stress and anxiety. The more balls you are juggling at a time, the more you need to worry about, and the more you stress. This can (and often does) create a vicious cycle of never-ending stress.

Suffice to say, multitasking is not quite as good for you as you were originally led to believe. But don't just take my word for it, there is actually research to back this up. Research published in the July 2017 issue of the journal Human Brain Mapping found that multitasking reduces productivity by as much as 40%[2], whereas another research by the American Psychological Association went further even further and concluded that mental overload caused by heavy duty multitasking can result in "catastrophe"[3].

So, avoid multitasking.

**Unitasking**

Now that you understand that multitasking isn't quite as effective as you (and most people really) have been led to believe, what you are left with is really one other option.

Enter Unitasking.

The concept of unitasking is not new. It just had been overtaken by the myth of multitasking being a more productive way to work.

The idea is simple - just focus on one thing at a time, and only move on to the next when you are done with that.

There are lots of benefits to this approach:

- When you focus on just one thing at a time, you drastically improve your chances of getting it done on time. If the thing you are working on has a strict deadline, unitasking is really the only way to go.

- Heard of the fabled "flow state", those rare moments when you are totally in the zone and work just flows? They are far easier to achieve when you are unitasking.

- Want a way to significantly reduce your levels of stress and anxiety? Try unitasking. Not having to worry about several things at one will do wonders to your stress levels.

As you can see, when you adopt the unitasking approach, you not only improve the quality of your work, you also benefit your health and well-being. What more reasons do you need?

**Moving forward**

If the quality and impact of your work are important (and your well-being), then you really should not consider multitasking. Avoid it where possible, and adopt this new paradigm - the paradigm of unitasking.

That said, if you have fallen into the habit of multitasking, don't beat yourself up over not knowing how it actually is counterproductive. Most people don't know. Hell, I learned it the hard way. I adopted multitasking as one of my key work strategies for many years. But then I learned better. And now, so do you.

Stop multitasking.

Start unitasking.

—

Understanding the fallacy of multitasking puts you in a great place to make the most of your time and energy. Next, we will look at a strategy for starting your day in the most impactful way, a strategy that unitasking supplements (and vice versa).

*We are what we repeatedly do. Excellence, then, is not an act but a habit - Aristotle*

# Chapter 5

## How To Start Your Day Right

The way you start your day has a significant impact on how productive you are. Actually, it has a significant on your whole day, both personal and work. So it should come as no surprise that starting your day right will have a massive impact on how effective you are.

So how can you start your day right, day in day out?

Enter: Morning systems.

**Morning systems?**

If you are familiar with my blog (mhasalek.com) then you know how big a fan I am of systems. Systems simplify things. They make you more effective. They cut down on time wastage. They help you become better. Systems are great, not just for business, but also for individuals.

Systems can help you improve your life.

By the way, if you are wondering whether morning systems have anything to do with routines, they absolutely do. But they are much more than routines, as you will find out later in this chapter. But let's look at some of the benefits of having an effective morning system first.

When you create a morning system, you basically automate how your morning plays out. This will benefit you in many ways.

- Having a morning system will stop you from trying to figure out how your morning will play out every single day. This saves you time. It cuts down on distractions, and procrastination.

- When you have a system for how you will start your day, you will have clarity, which cuts down on distractions and procrastination even further.

- Morning systems help you conserve your willpower and mental energy. As a 2014 study published in the journal Motivation Science[1] found, there is a limit on how many decisions you can make in a day, as they use up your willpower - the more decisions you make early on, the less mental energy you will have left for later/important stuff. Having a morning system automates a lot of decisions, which means you have more mental energy to focus on important things, like taking better care of yourself (according to the American Psychological Association's annual Stress in America Survey, most people said lack of willpower was the main reason for not making healthy lifestyle changes[2]).

- The other big benefit of having a system that you follow regularly is that it creates queues for your brain. So if your morning system includes starting work at 9 am every weekday, after a while you will struggle not to start work at 9 am. Your brain will become so used to this system that it will adopt it as a habit, an automated will become so used to this system that it will adopt it as a habit, an automated program. Pair that with your sequence (see below), and you will have an automated domino effect that will enable you to start your day in the strongest of footings with the smallest action.

- As a 2006 study[3] found, having a routine helps promote well-being, health, happiness, stress, and work-life balance. The beneficial impact of routines on anxiety and stress was further supported by a 2007 research[4], which found that participants who had experienced a major disaster were able to better cope and get on with their lives when they had a routine.

A system has the potential to magnify those benefits. It will not just positively impact your productivity and results now, but potentially for the rest of your life. Read on to learn how you can create an impactful, highly personalised, morning system.

The power of an effective morning system is incredible. I can't stress the benefits enough. An impactful morning system = an automated virtuous cycle that helps you start your day right, every day.

Now that you understand how useful and beneficial morning systems can be, let's look at how to develop one for you.

**Creating an effective and impactful morning system**

Now that you understand the benefits of having a good morning system, how do you go about creating one?

I would love to tell you that there is a hard and fast rule for this, but there really is not. No two person is the same. So only because my morning system works really well for me does not automatically mean it will work for you too.

So rather than giving you a standard morning system, I will give you the building blocks, and guidance for coming up with a system that works for you. I will guide you step by step, but what I will not do is spoon feed you. Teach a man to fish and all that...

Sounds good?

Great, let's get started.

**Step by step guide for creating your morning system**

Here are the steps for creating an impactful, personalised, morning system:

1. Create a No list - The creation of your morning routine should start by determining what you will NOT do. When devising a plan, it is just as important to know what not to do as it is to know what to do, if not more so. So start by creating a list of what you will not and should not do first thing in the morning. To help you get started, here is a question to ask yourself: what do you sometimes/ often do first thing in the morning that negatively impacts your productivity and your day/mood? Here is an obvious one - do not check your emails first thing in the morning. There are just too many reasons why it is a bad idea. But if you are not sold, do some research yourself to find out just why checking your email first thing in the morning is not a good idea.

2. Create a Yes list - Having a No list helps you get clarity on what not to do. It also helps you think about all the things you should do. So the second step is about

making a Yes list, a list of things you should do. Things that are good for you, things that will help you start your day strong. Here are some suggestions to get you started: meditation, journaling, exercise.

3. Plan the sequence - Now that you have your ultimate list of what will be part of your impactful morning system, it is important to decide on a sequence. This is one of the key ways my morning system differs from a standard routine. Understand this, if you want to make your system really work for you, you need to use it consistently. You need to systemise it. That will be a challenge unless you create an automated habit of doing it every day. Let's face it, we tend to forget things, and/or get distracted. So if you have to decide every day when you do what, some things will fall through the crack. The best way to avoid that is to automate it, and that can only happen when you know the sequence of what happens when. This is why it is not enough for you to just have a list of things to do. It is also the reason why a lot of people don't stick to routines. Use the list you have developed so far, then decide what you do first, second, and so on. Once you have a clear sequence, you have your morning system. Now all you need to do is implement it.

**Consistency**

Once you have your morning system, you are well on your way to starting your day strong. You will have a clear strategy, and a system to put into play.

Consistent application, though, is very important. Only by consistently applying your system will you automate it. Do it enough times, and you won't even have to think about the steps. Do it enough times, and it will become second nature, and that is when you reap the full rewards of your morning system.

**Trial and error**

One other thing to note about creating your impactful, personal morning system is the fact that the system you initially create is not necessarily going to be the best one, or the final one. When you apply your initial system a few times, you might find that some things don't work well for you, or the sequence needs to be changed, or that there are things you want to add or do differently.

The final version of your morning system will only come through trial and error. So it is important to be patient if your morning system does not work as well as you had hoped. Only because the initial version doesn't work very well, does not mean it doesn't work - if there are issues, try different things, and different ways. Keep trying until you have a version that works.

When I developed my original morning system, it did not work very well outright. Not because the plan wasn't sound, but because I found out that things often work differently in practice than they do in theory. So I tried different things, tried altering my sequence, until I ended up with a system that works. And even that I tweak from time to time.

There is also the fact that down the line, you will learn of things that you want to incorporate into your system. That's what happened when I incorporated my time-boxed list (see Chapter 7) to my morning system - it was not part of my original system.

Your morning system is dynamic. It is not written in stone, so change it as you see fit. Just don't change it too much, and not unless it really will benefit you.

By the way, remember what you read about Chronotype in chapter 3? Make sure your morning system works with your Chronotype, not against it.

**Moving forward**

Saying that morning systems help is a massive understatement, because they are incredibly powerful.

That said, you can take them further.

Once you get the hang of your morning system, why not create one for your evenings? Or your afternoon for that matter? These additional systems will further systemise your day, cut down on distractions even more, and make you even more effective.

Don't run before you can walk though, especially if you are new to routines and systems. Start by creating a morning system. Work out its kinks, make it really work for you.

Only then should you consider adding on more systems.

In the next chapter, we will look into a strategy that will help you maximise your work hours, reduce distractions, and deal with procrastination.

*There is virtue in work and there is virtue in rest. Use both and overlook neither* - Alan Cohen

# Chapter 6

## How 20 Minutes Can Transform Your Productivity

Dealing with distractions and procrastination is the biggest reasons why people struggle to be effective. Those factors cause a whole host of issues which ends up costing a lot of time with barely anything, if anything, to show for it.

And that's where the Pomodoro Technique can help.

**Pomodoro?**

Invented back in the late 80s by Francesco Cirillo, the Pomodoro Technique is a great strategy for dealing with distractions and procrastination. Here's the theory behind this technique - large tasks can be broken down into smaller segments called Pomodoro. Each separated by a short break.

The segmentation and breaks are designed to take advantage of our brain's short attention span.

The Pomodoro Technique can be great for improving your productivity. Not only is it good for dealing with our short attention spans, but it also makes it easier to do things by chucking them down. That makes them less intimidating.

Often we procrastinate because the task/project is too big and/or complex - so when it is broken down into smaller tasks, doing it gets a lot easier. Rather than committing to doing hours of work, all you really need to do is commit to just 25 minutes at a time (or less) - much easier won't you say?

Now that you know a bit about the Pomodoro technique, let's look at how it works.

**The original Pomodoro Technique**

The original Pomodoro technique involves working in 25-minute segments (or Pomodoro cycles as they are commonly called), with 5-minute breaks between each cycle.

The idea is to focus on what you are doing (and ignore other things), for the duration of those 25 minutes.

Once your 25 minutes is up you give yourself a break. This helps reboot your attention span. Then you do the same thing again.

Repeat four times (25-minute cycles followed by 5-minute breaks).

Then take a longer break for 20 minutes.

And then you start again, as long as you want to carry on.

It's simple, and it is a good strategy.

That said, things have changed, so you might need to make some tweaks to make this strategy work for you (even better).

We'll look into that next.

**Revised Pomodoro**

The original method is great, but things have changed since Cirillo first developed this strategy.

Our attention spans have shortened, significantly, and it keeps getting shorter.

Suffice to say, sticking with the original 25-minute format might not be quite as effective.

Based on the reality of our shorter attention spans, I suggest a revised Pomodoro technique. After all, only because something worked once does not mean it will always work. To make the most of something, we need to stay flexible and change when change is necessary.

That's what the Revised Pomodoro Technique is here to do.

Now that that's out of the way, let's get down to the brass tacks of how to make the revised technique work for you.

**How the Revised Pomodoro Technique works**

To start with, rather than opting for 25 minutes, start with 20-minute cycles.

Because you're working in shorter cycles, keep the breaks to around 2-3 minutes. Yes, it doesn't give you a lot of time, but that also means there's less risk of you losing focus and getting distracted.

After three Pomodoro cycles, take a longer break of about 15 minutes.

Now that you understand how the revised technique works, it is important for you to understand something - this is a guideline, not a hard and fast rule. Try the original 25-minute version, then try the revised 20-minute version. See which one works for you.

Once you have the version that works for you well, then you can test longer and shorter periods to come up with a version that works for you.

**Distractions**

The whole point of the Pomodoro technique is to do focused work, so it is absolutely essential for you to keep your distractions to a minimum. Zero distractions being the ideal scenario. As research[1] shows, the average office worker loses over an hour a day due to distractions - this adds up pretty fast. So if you want to be effective, it is really important that you limit your distractions.

Limiting your distractions is actually not that hard to do, especially when using the Pomodoro Technique. As you will only be working in short time windows, it will become easier to ignore things that might otherwise distract or interrupt you, like checking your phone and/or your email.

To get the most out of the Pomodoro Technique, you need to be strict about the no-distraction rule. Only focus on the task at hand and nothing else, during your Pomodoro cycle.

### Egg timer

Using an old-fashioned egg-timer is a great way to track your Pomodoro cycles and limit your distractions. A stop-watch or even the timer on your smartphone (or laptop) will work just as well.

That said, I suggest using an old-fashioned egg-timer/alarm clock.

Here's why: when you use a timer like that, you reduce your sources of distractions. If you are writing, for instance, and have your computer or phone around, they can easily distract you. Whereas when you use an analog tool like an egg-timer you significantly reduce your distractions. Distractions are one of the key reasons for procrastination, so you improve the quality of your work (as well as the probability of getting your work down on time) when you cut down distractions.

### Breaks

Now, more than ever, breaks are important. We live in the age of information. We are constantly being bombarded by information, be it on your phone, the computer, the TV or even the billboards (and smartboards) on the street. So it's good to just switch off every once in a while.

It's not just good for your brain, but also for your stress levels, creativity, productivity, happiness, and your overall sanity! A 1997 study published in the journal Ergonomics[2] found that people who took frequent short breaks were more productive than those who don't. It also found that those who took the breaks were healthier. The main focus of the study was people who continuously worked on computers - that is basically everyone these days.

But breaks are only good when they are used in a good way. As a study published in the American Journal of Preventative Medicine[3] found, work breaks often involve "health-compromising behaviours". Goes without saying then that if you want to make the most of your breaks, it is important to spend them well. That is what we will look at next.

### Five of the best ways to take breaks

So taking breaks is good for you. But what would be the best way to take those breaks?

There is no hard and fast rule for how you take your break, but here are five suggestions on what you can do to best spend your free time:

1. Meditate
2. Stretch
3. Walk
4. Exercise
5. Journal

**Meditate**

Meditation is one of the best ways to use your break, both short and long ones. It is a great way to centre yourself, as well as for reducing stress[4].

Meditation helps you to become calm. It also is a great way to get clarity on things. If you are confused about something, your next step for instance (or a problem that's bugging you), meditation can be a very useful way to come up with a solution.

Talk about an effective way to spend your break.

**Stretch**

Doing some stretching is another great use of your break time. Stretching helps improve your overall mobility and flexibility[5], and also is great for reducing injury.

If you are like most people and spend a lot of time at work sitting down, stretching will be a great way to counteract the problems that sitting for long periods causes[6].

Wondering what problems long periods of sitting causes? Here are a few (source - webmd):

1. Shortens your lifespan
2. Higher risk of heart problems
3. Increased risk of diabetes
4. Increased risk of DVT (deep vein thrombosis)

5. More likely to gain weight
6. Can increase anxiety levels
7. Damages your back
8. Increased risk of getting varicose veins
9. Increased risk of cancer

Suffice to say, sitting for long periods of time is not good for you. So if you have some spare time, stretching will be a great way to use them.

**Walk**

Walking around a bit is a great use of your break time. You can just stretch your legs for a bit during your short breaks. During the longer ones, you can even go for a stroll outside.

Being in nature is a great way to increase your happiness[7], as well as reduce your stress and anxiety levels. As an April 2019 research found, spending 20 minutes in contact with nature significantly lowers your stress hormone levels[8]. So those longer breaks that come after four Pomodoro cycles are ideal for practising this. This way not only will you boost your productivity level, you will also reduce your stress levels, improve your happiness levels and give your overall well-being a boost[9].

Here's another reason why taking a walk outside is a good idea: our brains function less effectively in stuffy rooms because of carbon dioxide buildup. Taking a walk outside helps eliminate that sluggish effect and helps you feel more awake and alert.

By the way, I understand that there will be times when you can't go out for a walk during your break. Here's the good news - you don't have to go outside for a walk to reap some of the benefits.

A 2014 Stanford research[10] found that people who spent time on a treadmill during their breaks experienced up to a 60% increase in their creativity. This is 60% more than people who spent their breaks sitting down.

The research also found that the creativity boost from the walk lasted several hours.

Talk about a win-win way to take a break...

**Exercise**

The benefits of exercise are pretty well-documented, but did you know that it also has a big impact on your productivity levels and effectiveness? A Briston University study[11] found that exercise improved productivity levels in their study participants by an impressive 21%! That is a sizable improvement won't you say.

So exercise is good for you - not just for your health, but also for your productivity. But does that mean you need to spend an hour in the gym every day? That won't fit with the break schedules...

Here's the thing - even a moderate amount of exercise can be really good for you. Heard of HIIT? It's an exercise strategy that involves doing really short periods of high-intensity workout, and the benefits are often the same (if not better) than longer, moderate (and low) intensity workouts.

So whether you have 20 minutes, 5 minutes (or less), you can fit in some exercise.

**Journal**

Journaling (or keeping a diary) is a great way to spend your breaks. It is a great way to clear your head, and is also a very effective way to deal with your thoughts, emotions, and challenges.

From just a productivity point of view, journaling can be very useful for boosting your effectiveness as it can help you to limit your distractions (by limiting the chatter inside your head), and get clarity. But it does have a lot more benefits.

Journaling helps develop self-awareness - the awareness that is absolutely essential for personal growth. It helps you identify your strengths and weaknesses, which helps you get better. And it is one of the best tools for improving your mental health and well-being[12].

**What not to do**

There are lots of ways to spend your breaks well, but here is something you should avoid: start something that will take longer to finish than your break duration.

So if you are tempted to check Facebook or play games on your phone, avoid the temptations. They will distract you, and it will be really easy to lose your momentum.

**Bonus tip**

There will be times when motivating yourself will be hard. Especially for those times, here is a bonus tip that will really help: assign a mini-reward for yourself that you will get once you have finished the Pomodoro cycle.

When you do this, you will have added motivation to finish the work, as you will be looking forward to the reward, e.g., checking your phone (yes, most of us love the dopamine hit we get from checking our phones).

There is another reason why this works really well - this will stop you from doing/getting something you are really craving (maybe that nice cup of cappuccino?) until you have finished your cycle, which motivates you to get your work done. This strategy works as both carrot and stick - you get the reward when you reach your goal, but you also miss out on the reward if you don't reach your goal.

If you are struggling or need some extra motivation, try this out.

**Flow state**

One of the side effects of the Pomodoro Technique often is getting into the flow state. When that happens, carry on. Don't stop after your time is up. Continue as long as you want to.

The timer is there as a guide to facilitate your work, and not as a limiter. So if you get into the "zone", do not let it interrupt you.

**Moving forward**

The Pomodoro Technique is a great way to deal with distractions, procrastination and for boosting your overall productivity.

But it will only work if you apply it, consistently. Give it a fair shot before dismissing it.

In that regard, I want you to do something right now - put it on your list to try the Pomodoro Technique today, and/or tomorrow, and try it consistently for at least seven days.

Knowledge without application doesn't amount to much, so apply what you have learned here to get the most benefit.

—

In the next chapter, we will explore a strategy for managing your time effectively. The strategy will be a great complement to the Pomodoro Technique we've covered here, and it will make you a master at managing your time. If you struggle with time management, you absolutely need to read it.

Let's continue.

You will never "find" time for anything. If you want time, you must make it - Charles Bruxton

# Chapter 7

## Planning Your Time Effectively

You have covered about half of the book so far, so congratulations on your perseverance. So far you have learned about three of the biggest productivity myths and how to counter them. You have also learned how to start your day right and a 20-minute strategy that can effectively deal with procrastination and distractions.

Now we will look at a strategy that will put you firmly in charge of your time. If you struggle with time management, this just might be the strategy you need to end that struggle once and for all.

Enter: timeboxing

**Boxing time?**

The concept is actually fairly simple: plan out your working hours in specific time increments, or boxes. So if your timeboxes are an hour-long, your average workday will look something like this:

- 9-10am
- 10-11
- 11-12
- 12-1pm
- 1-2
- 2-3
- 3-4
- 4-5

### 5-minute increments

Two of the most successful people in the world use timeboxing to plan their days: Elon Musk and Bill Gates[1].

They plan out their days in 5-minute increments.

That level of specificity, however, is not for everyone - especially for someone new to this strategy. Only because a certain method or way of doing things works for someone does not, by default, mean that it will work for everyone.

So, if you are wondering whether you should start following Musk's suit and plan your day out in 5-minute increments, my answer is a big NO.

That would be counterproductive for anyone who is new to timeboxing.

Walk before you can run.

Start slow.

Start with timeboxes of an hour or more, and then narrow down later, once you are really familiar with the strategy.

### How I use timeboxing

I use timeboxing every day, first thing in the morning, and use it to schedule my day. I use my weekly plan as a guideline to then plan out exactly what I will do and when.

This is also a way for me to do some reality checks and make sure that I allocate enough time to each of my main goals for the day.

In case you are wondering, I usually plan my days in 20-60 minute increments. That suits my style and complements my Revised Pomodoro Technique.

All said it is important to be mindful of your own needs. So when planning your timeboxed work schedule, schedule timeboxes in increments that work for you. And the best way to figure out what will work for you is to try out different durations/time increments.

**86,400 seconds**

Imagine a bank that deposits £86,400 into your account at the start of each day. At the end of every day, the bank gets rid of whatever cash you did not use that day - no balance is carried over to the next day.

In a situation like that, what would you do?

You would withdraw every single penny, right? You would be nuts not to!

That's actually how time works.

At the start of each day, you get 86,400 seconds, and at the end of every day, all of that is reset. Whatever time you used well was well-spent - the rest of it is lost forever.

**Time is a valuable resource**

To understand the value of one-second, ask someone who avoided getting into an accident by a mere second.

To understand the value of one minute, ask someone who missed their flight by a mere minute.

To understand the value of one hour, ask a student who was an hour late in submitting his assignment.

To understand the value of one week, ask the creator of a weekly podcast.

To understand the value of one month, ask the editor of a monthly magazine.

To understand the value of one year, ask a researcher who missed his annual grant application date.

Every moment matters.

Your life is shaped based on how you use the 86,400 seconds you get every day. Choose to use them wisely, because once they're gone, they are gone forever.

**Moving forward**

Two of the biggest problems with time management are: underestimating the amount of time you will need for doing a task and not having any clarity on what happens when. Both of those factors result in confusion and distraction, and ultimately, bad time management.

Timeboxing is a great strategy for dealing with both of those. In fact, it helps minimise work overload, which has been found to decrease productivity by 68% in people who feel they just don't have enough hours in the day to finish all their tasks[2].

Timeboxing also has a positive impact on decision making, as a 2009 study by the Systems Research Forum found[3].

Timeboxing is a great tool to add to your toolbox. But like any new tool, it will take some practice to really get used to it and make the most of it. But if you stick with it (and successfully adopt it), it will transform your ability to manage your time effectively, and will also have a massive impact on your productivity and results.

—-

When you start using timeboxing, you will usually find that there isn't enough time in the day to do everything you want to do. You will need to be selective. As important as managing your time is, unless you have clarity on what you should focus your time on you won't be doing impactful work. That is not effective time management. And that's where the strategy in the next chapter comes in.

Read on.

*You've gotta keep control of your time, and you can't unless you say no. You can't let people set your agenda in life* - Warren Buffet

# Chapter 8

## Planning For Impact

In this chapter, we will look at another important aspect of radical productivity - prioritisation.

Let's face it, there just aren't enough hours in a day to do all the things we want to do. Generally, the number of things you want to do in a day will require way more than the 24 hours you have. So learning to be selective about what you spend your time on is one of the key tenets of being radically productive.

Enter: the 80/20 rule

**The 80/20 Rule**

The 80/20 rule (also known as the Pareto principle), is a popular concept. From a productivity perspective, here is the basic concept behind that rule: 80% of your results come from 20% of your work.

Generally, that rule applies to nearly every type of work, and in every industry. But don't take my word for it - review the results you have had over the last month. What percentage of your work contributed to the lion's share of the results?

The point is this - some tasks will always be more impactful than others. A small number of tasks will always be of higher value than the rest.

The more high-impact work you do, the more impactful you are. And vice versa. Ever felt like you just work and work but get nowhere? That's the result of focusing on and prioritising low-impact work.

Because you only have a limited number of hours every day, you need to prioritise. You need to be selective about what you will spend your time on. So use the 80/20 principle to select the highest value tasks, and then make those your primary focus. Get those done first, and focus on the rest if you have time left.

There are lots of reasons why you need to prioritise - here are a few of them:

- Prioritising usually leads to you playing to your strengths, and doing the things that you are best at. The work that has the most impact usually is work that you are really good at. This is good for businesses too, as a Gallup study found that employees who exercised their strengths on a regular basis are 8% more productive and 6 times more likely to be engaged

- When you start focusing your attention on the 20% of the important stuff, you will also start to filter out the 80% of the stuff that isn't that important, especially the also start to filter out the 80% of the stuff that isn't that important, especially the distractions. Do this regularly, and you will build up your mental muscle for focusing on the important stuff, which in turn will make you more impactful in the long term. Remember, getting clarity, and deciding what not to do is just as important as deciding what to do.

- Remember about the limit there is to our mental energy (see Chapter 5)? Prioritising means you limit the number of decisions you have to make, which limits the amount of mental energy you need to use. This is really important if you want to stay at your peak and do focused work. Depleting your mental energy on low-impact work will detrimentally affect your ability to do the high-impact work, so prioritisation is essential.

- Here's yet another reason why you need to prioritise - if you don't, you will find your schedule being dictated by the requests (and demands) from other people. How you spend your time will then largely be determined by others, rather than by you. Guess how useful that is for doing impactful work...

To summarise, it is not just important but essential, to prioritise the 20% of your highest value tasks.

By the way, in case you are thinking that you can sacrifice your sleep to get even more hours, do not do that. As I learned the hard way, that's a really bad idea. Do not sacrifice your sleep to get more done, as that is always counterproductive (review Chapter 3 if you need a refresher on the importance of proper sleep).

**How to find your 20% (or, what should you prioritise)**

It should be pretty clear by now that prioritising plays a vital role in having impact, and being radically productive. But you might be wondering about how to come up with your 20% tasks to prioritise, and about what you should or should not put on the top of your list. Sometimes it can be a bit challenging to choose.

That's where Eisenhower's Urgent/Important principle comes in.

It is a simple yet effective principle that will help you simplify the process of prioritising. The idea is simple - focus on things that are important, and urgent, first. Using that principle, your tasks will fit into these four categories (1 = highest priority, 4 = lowest priority):

1. Important and urgent
2. Important but not urgent
3. Urgent but not important
4. Not urgent and not important

Use the Eisenhower Decision Grid to help.

You can draw a similar grid to the one showed in the next page to help you identify which tasks fit where. Draw one in the space below and create your own prioritised list as you follow along.

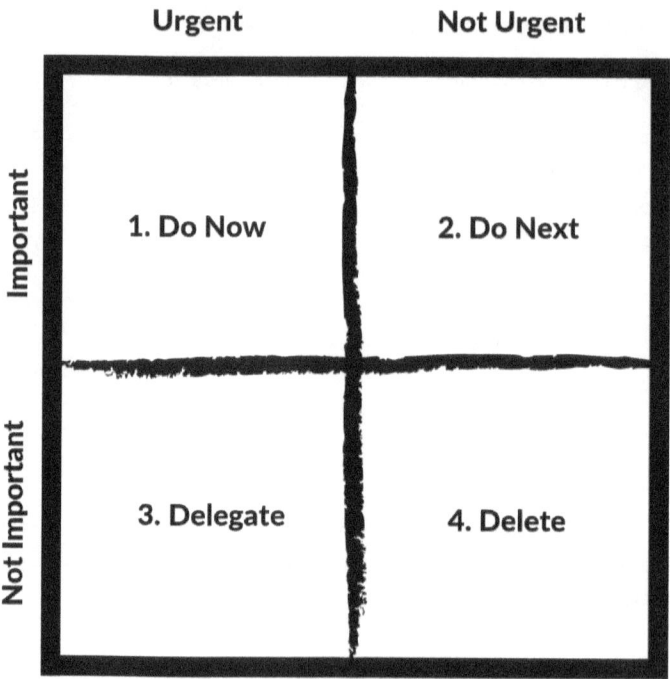

**The Eisenhower Decision Grid**

Here is how it works:

1.  Do now - Tasks that fit into this section are things that need to be done now, pronto. Don't delay them. These are of primary concern.

2.  Do next - Tasks that fit into this section are high impact, high-value tasks. These might not have any urgency attached to them, but they will be things that will make a big difference down the line. This can be something like finally writing that book you've always wanted to write, or doing the training that you know will have a big impact on your work and/or life. Only because they are not urgent does not mean they should be delayed. The sooner you get to them, the better, so do these as soon as possible.

3. Delegate - The tasks that fit into this third section are things that you can delegate fairly easily. See below for more on delegation.

4. Delete - When you prioritise your tasks, you will realise that not everything on your list actually needs to be done. You need to be smart with your time and energy, which means some things just do not deserve your time and energy. So let them go. This will also help you free up time and energy to focus on the let them go. This will also help you free up time and energy to focus on the important and impactful stuff.

If you have a huge list of things to do, use the above list to figure out what you need to prioritise, and create your 80/20 list.

Then focus on the 20%.

Any time you get stuck prioritising or you're a bit unclear, just remember the four Ds:

1. Do now
2. Do next
3. Delegate
4. Delete

We will look next at ways to deal with the non-priority 80% of the tasks.

**What to do with the remaining 80%**

When you are choosing to focus on the 20% of your highest-impact work, you are not completely saying no to everything else. What you are doing is being selective about what you prioritise.

That said, some things you will not end up having the time or the energy for because let's face it, you only have so much time and energy in a day, and there is always too much to do.

So here is what you can do with the remaining 80% (the low impact work):

1. Do some of them, but only after you've done the high impact work - This is mainly for things that aren't high impact per se, but are important,

nonetheless. So things like paying your bills, dealing with your mortgage and taxes, etc will fit into this category. Just be mindful of not letting them take up too much of your time, because important as these tasks are they don't actually help you progress. And you can't have impact, or be radically productive, if you are not moving forward.

2. Delegate - Delegation is one of the best ways to deal with all the things that you do not have the time and/or energy for. Delegation, in fact, is one of the best ways to increase your capacity and ability to be radically productive. This can be as casual as sharing some tasks with your partner (or friends even), or as structured as having an assistant (or virtual assistant). Just be clear about what needs to be done and let someone else take care of it, enabling you to stop worrying about the task(s).

3. Do later - There will always be things that you want to do that don't actually need to be done now. Either they are not important or not impactful, or they can just wait till later. So, create a list of all such things, and come back to them later, when you have the time and energy. Just do a braindump of anything and everything that you want to do but are not a priority (or important) at this point in time, then stop thinking about them and focus on the tasks at hand.

4. Let go - There will always be things that you want to do that don't actually need to be done. Just let them go. Saying no to things is a big part of effectively prioritising, and being effective.

**Delegate**

As I mentioned above, delegation is one of the best ways to do impactful work. And I really cannot stress enough just how useful this practice is. But don't just take my word for it - think about any one of your idols, someone at the top of their game, or someone you really admire. Does this person really do everything himself/herself?

People who do impactful work, people who are peak performers, people who are the best of the best, understand the value of delegation. They understand that they just can't be the best if they try to divide their focus amongst every big and small task. By delegating, they free up their time and energy to focus on what is truly important, and valuable. They focus on the 20%.

Still not convinced? Then how about this - do you really believe that someone like Elon Musk or Bill Gates or Richard Branson does everything on their own? They would not be where they are if they did not learn to delegate. Peak performers have teams behind them for good reason. Now you might not be as busy as they are, but if you want to have impact, you need to stop trying to do everything yourself.

You need to learn how to delegate.

**Dealing with emails**

I had to say something about emails, because emails are a big part of how we work now. Not just work, they are also a big part of our lives.

But they are also one of the biggest time hogs.

As a study[2] found, the average person spends around 13 hours a week of their work time on emails alone, which means 28% of their workweek is taken up by email! That does not include the time people spend on personal emails...

Emails are definitely a great way to communicate, but unless you manage them effectively they will eat up huge amounts of your time and energy. So when it comes to prioritising, factoring in (and managing effectively) your emails is really important.

To get you started, here are five tips for you to manage your emails effectively (and not let them become massive time hogs):

1. Do not check your emails first thing in the morning - If you do, your schedule will basically be dictated by others, and it is a really bad way to start your day. Refer to Chapter 5 if you need a refresher on how to start your day effectively.

2. Deal with your emails once or twice a day - This was something I first learned from Tim Ferriss' Four Hour Workweek. Tim actually has some pretty good tips and hacks for managing emails (and work + life), but this one, in particular, is a great rule to follow. Designate a specific time in the day for checking your email (I usually do it around 1 or 2 pm) and stick with that. It will get some time to get used to this schedule, but this can boost your effectiveness significantly. Not just

that, reducing the number of times you check your emails can also significantly cut down on your stress levels, as a University of British Columbia found[3]. So cutting down on how many times you check your email is not just good for your productivity levels, it is also good for your overall well-being.

3. Prioritise your emails - Every email you get does not need to be read, at least not immediately. Keep that in mind next time you check your inbox. Remember, 80/20... Read only the emails that are relevant, and important, which will be about 20% of your emails. Defer, or delete, the rest.

4. Set a time limit - Put a limit on the amount of time you will spend on emails. Remember the 13 hour stat from earlier? You risk becoming part of that statistic if you don't limit the amount of time you spend on emails.

5. Use the one-minute rule - Any email that can be responded to in a minute or less, respond right away. If you let them hang around in your inbox, coming back to them will just take up additional energy, and time. Better to just deal with them then and there, wherever possible. You can even use the "send later" feature to schedule your messages in case you want the other person to receive your response at a particular time.

Bonus tip: If you want an effective system for dealing with your emails (and managing email overwhelm), look up "Inbox Zero." There is a lot of free information out there on the topic to help you develop your own Inbox Zero strategy. If you still need help, feel free to reach out.

**Moving forward**

One of the most common complaints of the current era is not having enough time. What with all the developments, there is now more to do than ever. But despite the issues with time management, far too many people waste hours of their time on meaningless stuff. This is a sure sign that prioritisation is a critically important skill to have because when you learn how to prioritise your time, you will have clarity on what your time should and should not be spent on.

Being able to prioritise effectively is one of the key skills for being radically productive. There will always be more things to do than we have the time and energy for so this is not just a useful skill, it is a necessary one.

If you want to do work that matters, you have to prioritise. Without prioritising you will always be doing things that have little to no impact. You will be tired, exhausted, and frustrated. You will be running around doing lots of things, but with little to nothing to show for it. So learn to prioritise.

It will transform your productivity.

---

Even with all that you have learned so far, there will be times when you just don't feel like doing much (if anything). There will be times when you procrastinate. It happens to the best of us. In the next chapter, you will learn of a strategy that will help you to make the most of even such times.

Read on.

*If you spend too much time thinking about a thing, you'll never get it done - Bruce Lee*

# Chapter 9

## How To Be Productive Even When You're Lazy

There will be times when you just don't feel like doing anything. Times when you procrastinate.

Happens to everyone.

But only because there are times when we procrastinate does not mean those times have to be a complete waste.

That's where my strategy for productive procrastination comes in.

The idea is simple - during the times you procrastinate, do things that will move you forward but yet are easy to do.

**Creating a Productive Procrastination List**

Productive procrastination starts by creating a list of all the things you can do during the times that you are procrastinating.

Ideally these will be things that don't require much thinking on your part (decluttering, for example), things that you have fun doing (workout, perhaps), things that help you get out of the procrastination zone (e.g., shower), things that help you restart (e.g., meditation, workout), and so on.

The key here is to do something that will benefit you, but you won't struggle to do.

**15 ideas for your Productive Procrastination List**

By now you have a basic understanding of the Productive procrastination strategy. Now I will give you some concrete ideas for things you can include in your Productive procrastination list, to help solidify the concept for you and get you started on creating your own list.

1. Meditate - Meditation is by far one of the best ways to restart your brain. There are lots of advantages to meditating, and as such makes it an ideal thing to do when you don't really feel like working.

2. Go for a walk - This is similar to meditation. Walking outdoors has also been proven to have creativity boosting effects.

3. Have a shower - I often get my best ideas in the shower, and I am not the only one. This can be a great way to restart yourself.

4. Workout - 3 to 5 minutes of HIIT can do wonders for your concentration and creativity.

5. Brainstorm - if you are struggling to work, spend some time brainstorming about all the things that can do for the project at hand. This will be a great distraction and the ideas you get , etc., will be useful later on.

6. Declutter - Often clutter is one of the biggest reasons for procrastination, and that makes it an ideal candidate for the productive procrastination list.

7. Listen to a podcast - listen to a podcast that can help you.

8. Watch a TEDTalk - same principle as above.

9. Read - you can read a book or articles that will be useful. I am not recommending fiction books here because those can be a bit too distracting, and sort of defeats the purpose of productive procrastination.

10. Journaling - Journaling can be a great way to empty your mind of all that's going on. It is a great way to clear your head, and also really good for thinking out loud. It might even give you the clarity you need to stop procrastinating.

11. Proofread your content - if you have written things, proofreading and editing your work is a great way to productively procrastinate.

12. Come up with new ideas - this is a strategy I learned from James Altucher. The point of the exercise is to give your idea muscle a workout and come up with at least 10 new ideas every day. Great way to productively procrastinate.

13. Come up with ideas for your current project.

14. Learn a new language - Apps like Duolingo has made it really simple to learn languages in your spare time. You can do this for 5-10 minutes, or longer, or shorter.

15. Clear your email inbox - Clearing up your inbox is a great way to use times when you don't feel like doing much. This way you will have less to distract you later, as dealing with email is one of the biggest distractions around. Why not use the time to put into play some of the tips you learned about managing email in the last chapter?

**Moving forward**

Procrastination has been synonymous with wasting time for far too long. But only because you do not feel like doing one thing does NOT mean you don't feel like doing anything. Often doing something else, something simple and useful, can be just what you need to start again. This is a great way to productively use the times when you are struggling to do your work.

You can procrastinate and still be productive, by learning how to productively procrastinate. Yet another strategy, when adopted, that will radically improve your productivity.

Give it a shot.

—-

Productive procrastination is a great strategy for dealing with your procrastination. But there will be times when you procrastinate but really cannot afford do. Times when you just need to get things done, times when you have a deadline to meet. Pomodoro (chapter 6) certainly helps, but in the next chapter, we will explore another strategy that will help you to get things done even when you are struggling with procrastination.

Read on.

*The way to get started is to quit talking and begin doing - Walt Disney*

# Chapter 10

## Dealing With Procrastination: The Five-Minute Technique

You have come a long way in your radical productivity journey. So far you have learned about some of the biggest productivity myths and how to deal with them; you have learned how to determine the best time for you to start your day and how to do it effectively (and even how to systemise it for maximum effectiveness); you have learned about Pomodoro, about time boxing, about prioritisation, as well as about productive procrastination - and how to use those strategies to massively improve productivity and results. So when I say you have come a long way, I do not say it lightly.

In this chapter, we are going to explore a strategy that just might spell the end of procrastination.

Let's face it, procrastination is a big problem. And I do mean big: it costs businesses millions. It impacts career progression, job satisfaction, work-life balance, and even personal happiness. Based on how significantly procrastination affects a person, the impact can be severe. In fact, according to some researchers, the rate of procrastination has more than quadrupled in the last 30 years[1]!

So having a strategy that can help you beat procrastination can be extremely useful, it goes without saying.

Enter: my five-minute technique for beating procrastination.

**Why do we procrastinate?**

Before we get into the five-minute technique, it is important to understand that causes procrastination. As research has found, two of the biggest reasons why people procrastinate is:
i. Overwhelm.

ii. Not being in the right mood.

Let's break them down a bit.

Overwhelm - People often procrastinate because they get overwhelmed. There just doesn't seem to be enough time to get everything done, and/or the task seems too intimidating, which leads to people stressing about the task, and causes delays.

The thinking pattern goes something like this: "there is so much to do, and not enough time, how will I get it done? > I don't know how to get it all done in time > there isn't enough time."

This leads to even more delays, and procrastination, and stress. Often this becomes a full-blown vicious cycle of stress, which is why procrastination is such a big becomes a full-blown vicious cycle of stress, which is why procrastination is such a big cause of stress[2].

Wrong mood - Not being in the right mood is one of the other big causes of procrastination[3]. People don't feel like doing something, so they delay the task and wait to be in the right mood.

Often this goes on for a long time, and can even lead to habitual procrastination. As a 2010 research published in The Journal of Social Psychology[4] found, motivation (and self-regulation) is one of the biggest factors that cause procrastination.

So now you have some insight into why we procrastinate, let's find out how the five-minute technique can help.

**The Five Minute Technique**

The beauty of the five-minute technique lies in its simplicity.

Here's how it works: whatever you are procrastinating on, just commit to doing five minutes of it. It doesn't matter how complex the task, it can always be broken down into small chunks. Even if it cannot, you can always just do five minutes of it, and then take it from there.

Here's why it works: Nearly always getting started is the biggest hurdle, so when you do just five minutes of a task, you give yourself an easy, practical, doable way to get over the biggest hurdle. Remember how overwhelm is on of the key causes of procrastination? Starting small gets you over that hurdle.

The other reason why the five-minute technique is effective is because doing something for five minutes helps you stop worrying about being in the right mood. The right or wrong mood is more of an issue when you are thinking about doing a big piece of work. But if your commitment is just five minutes, it gets vastly easier to bypass the whole "not in the right mood" objection.

The key strength of the five-minute technique is the size of the commitment required. Doing a big task that can take hours can be intimidating, but doing just five minutes of work on it is a lot less intimidating, if intimidating at all.

And that's not the end of it - one of the best side effects of the five-minute technique is how it usually leads to a snowball effect. Once you get started, it will be really easy to do another five minutes of work, and then another, and before you know it you will be on a roll. It gets easier to carry on with the task, once you get the ball rolling.

This can (and will) help you beat procrastination.

**Moving forward**

Understand this, no matter how effective a strategy is, it will only be effective when it is applied. So is the five-minute technique going to magically eliminate procrastination for you?

No, it will not.

But it certainly can go a long way in beating your procrastination habits, IF you apply it consistently.

And that's a key point to understand - procrastination is a habit, one you can train yourself to get rid of.

That said, it will take time and perseverance. If you are a serial procrastinator, this is a habit you have built up over many years, so it will not disappear overnight. That is why the five-minute technique is so effective, as the commitment is so small. Committing to doing just five minutes of a piece of work that you are procrastinating on is far easier than committing to getting through all of it.

If you are procrastinating on a task, you are struggling, so make things easy on yourself. Do not use the whole "I will do it later" as a rationale to get out of doing it.

As a 2011 study[5] found, that is one of the main reasonings used by people who procrastinate.

So start small. Do just five minutes of it. Then take it from there.

Procrastination is a growing problem[6], but this simple habit can end the negative cycle of procrastination, stress, anxiety, and shame for you. So it is well worth trying out won't you say?

—-

Being able to deal with procrastination will have a significant impact on your productivity and results. You are well on your way to radically improving your productivity. In the next chapter, we will take this one step further and look at a strategy that will help you turn small actions into big results. This is essential if you want to be radically productive over the long haul.

Let's continue.

*Success is the sum of small efforts, repeated day in and day out - Robert Collier*

# Chapter 11

## Focusing On The Long Term, One Step At A Time

One of the key things I want you to understand about radical productivity is this - it is not a short-term strategy. When I decided to write this book, I wanted to develop a framework that will not just help you become radically productive now, but will also help you stay radically productive for the rest of your life.

And the strategy we are going to explore in this chapter plays a big role in that - it is a big piece of the puzzle.

Think about something you are good at, and I mean really good at. How long did it take you to get really good at it?

Not overnight right?

This is a key principle to understand - sustainable, impactful progress does not happen overnight. If you want to get really good at something, it will happen gradually, through consistent effort, and that is the basis of incremental progress, the strategy we are going to learn about in this chapter.

**Incremental progress?**

You have heard of the phrase "slow and steady wins the race" right? That's the principle behind the strategy of incremental progress.

The idea is simple: do something small, regularly.

Research has shown that even small progress can boost our performance[1].

But it's not just about what research shows - the impact that incremental progress can have is all around is. You are the best case study of all - the person you are today, the achievements you have had to date, all that you have learned and experienced... none of that happened overnight. It all happened incrementally.

In every area where you have made significant progress, you will see the presence of incremental progress: you did something to move you forward and did so consistently, and that then added up to the progress down the line.

Small progress, taking things one step at a time, is also a smart way to learn as a 2016 study[2] found. The study observed science and maths teachers and found that teaching one thing at a time is a more effective method than teaching several things at a time.

No matter the area of life and/or work, incremental progress is effective.

In the same way your major achievements were a culmination of incremental progress, so were the achievement of basically everyone.

The concept is not new - we use it all the time. The point is to use it by design so that you can actively keep moving forward.

**Incremental progress plan (Or, how to make it work for you)**

Now that you understand the power of incremental progress, let's look at how you can make it work for you.

It starts by creating an incremental progress plan.

Follow the steps below to create your own:

1. Think about your big goal or the goal you want to achieve down the line. Define it as clearly as possible.

2. Brainstorm all that needs to happen, and all the steps you will need to take, to make that goal happen. Break them down as much as possible. By the way, you do not have to do something different every day - the idea is to do something regularly that helps you move forward, even if it is the same sort of task (see the example below if this point isn't absolutely clear).

3. Now create a daily list for the next 6 months to 1 year (or more), assigning 1 mini goal per day. You can definitely include more, but if time or energy is limited, then even one goal a day is good. Remember, the key isn't to try and get everything done overnight but rather to make small, consistent progress

which will add up. One other thing to note about the daily/regular goals is this: don't try to do too much. That can overwhelm you and can make it hard for you to keep at it. So stick to a goal that you can do regularly, day in day out, without being overwhelmed.

Example incremental progress plan:

1. Goal: Write a 10,000-word book

2. Incremental tasks: write 100-1,000 words a day (what your daily/regular target will be will depend on what you are going to be able to get done without being overwhelmed).

3. Plan: At a rate of 1,000 words a day, it will take 10 days to finish the book, whereas 100 words a day will require 100 days. But even 100 days for accomplishing this goal is not something to sneeze at.

I'm going to give you a real-life example of how incremental progress works, and use this very book as the subject. When I decided to write this book, my goal was to write just one chapter a day. This meant that I could do all the other things I needed to do but still make progress with my book. Often I ended up writing more than that, but the goal was simple - just one chapter a day. That made it a challenging goal, but not overwhelming, and ensured that I kept to it even on days when I didn't really feel motivated to write (the other strategies I have talked about so far also helped).

Here's the key to making incremental progress work for you: focus on the action, not the result. Just keep doing the work, do it consistently, and it will add up in the end.

**Be like the ant**

Do you know the story of the ant and the grasshopper?

It goes something like this: there once was an ant and a grasshopper. The grasshopper spent all his time playing and having fun, while the ant worked day in day out to build up his reserve of food. The grasshopper teased the ant all the time, but that did not stop the ant from doing his work.

Then a long, bitter winter came.

Everything froze over.

There was no sign of food anywhere.

The ant survived through the bitter winter thanks to the reserve he had built up. The grasshopper though had no food and wasn't so fortunate.

The moral of the story is that the ones who persevere and put in the effort are the ones who make progress (and survive). The ant had to put in effort consistently, incrementally, to build up the reserve that helped him get through the long winter. It just would not have been possible for him to build up that reserve overnight.

Had it not been for his incremental progress, he would not have survived.

If you want to be radically productive, if you want your work to matter, if you want to have an impact, you need to be like the ant. You need to put in the effort consistently. It is not enough to do some work and then stop - to make progress and have a real impact, you need to keep at it.

Consistency matters. Incremental progress adds up.

**Moving forward**

Seth Godin makes a really good point about the impact of incremental progress: "The thing is, incremental daily progress (negative or positive) is what actually causes transformation. A figurative drip, drip, drip. Showing up, every single day, gaining in strength, organizing for the long haul, building connection, laying track — this subtle but difficult work is how culture changes."

In many ways, incremental progress is like gardening. You plant the seeds. You nurture them. Then over time, those seeds grow into beautiful plants that bear fruits and flowers.

Incremental progress is all about planting those seeds and nurturing them by taking consistent steps which will then bear fruit and bring lots of benefits for you down the line. But try to do too much at once, and you will often wear yourself out - in the same way over-watering plants does not make them stronger, it usually makes them weaker.

Consistent regular effort matters, as growth is a marathon, not a sprint. Rome really was not built in a day. Small steps forward, taken consistently, do add up.

Create an incremental progress plan.

Adopting this principle will transform your long-term impact and your life.

—-

Incorporating incremental progress into your mindset will go a long way in creating long-lasting and impactful results for you. This is very important for the long term. In the next chapter we will explore another concept which will further augment incremental progress and supercharge your progress and productivity, in the long term.

*Without continual growth and progress, such words as improvement, achievement, and success have no meaning - Benjamin Franklin*

# Chapter 12

## How To Keep Getting Better

Do you know what one of the key differences is between people who do incredible things and the rest of the population?

They are not complacent.

They keep growing, and improving.

Think of any one of your favourite sports or business personalities, someone who is at the top of their game. They all continually work on themselves and their skills, in order to get better. They are where they are because of this ethos. Being the best isn't easy, and happens only when you commit to continuous growth and improvement.

And that is what Kaizen is all about.

**Kaizen?**

Kaizen's roots lie in Japanese management and is one of the key contributors to the success of major businesses like Toyota. Adopting Kaizen enabled them to get better and better, and always be one step ahead. And that is what Kaizen can do for you too.

But before we learn more about Kaizen, here are some important things to understand about radical productivity and peak performance:

Not continuously growing and improving can cause you to become outdated. Things are always changing - if you don't keep up, you will fall behind.

Not focusing on growth and improvement can make you complacent. Only because something worked in the past does not mean it will always work, and the only way to know what still works (and will work in the future) is to keep improving.

There are always better ways of doing things. But you will never discover them if you don't commit to growth and improvement.

If you don't grow and improve regularly, you will lose your edge.

If you want to be the best, if you want to be at the top of your game, if you want to be one step ahead (of your competitors) and be a peak performer, adopting Kaizen is essential.

**Using Kaizen**

Kaizen is more of a mindset than a step by step set of rules. It's all about committing to grow and improve continuously and do so consistently.

Continuity and consistency are both important, as one without the other won't make the endeavour quite as effective.

When you are growing and improving yourself, you can only get the most out of it if you do so every opportunity you get and do so consistently (rather than once in a while, as an afterthought).

**Consistency**

The importance of consistency, when it comes to Kaizen really cannot be overstressed. Remember what you learned about incremental progress, and what made it such an effective strategy? That's the power of consistency - doing things consistently means they will add up over time.

Doing so inconsistently (as and when you feel like it) will make it easy for you to forget and/or get distracted, and before long you will get complacent.

If you want to reap the benefits of Kaizen, you need to make it a way of life. That is if being radically productive is what you are after.

**Staying ahead**

Kaizen isn't just beneficial for growth and improvement. It is also important if you want to keep up with the latest developments.

We live in a time of rapid changes and disruptions - things are always changing, and often really fast. So unless you are up to date on things that impact your skills and effectiveness, you will lose your edge.

You will stop being radically productive.

But when you commit to continuously grow and improve, the new developments will be easier to keep up with, and it will be easier for you to stay ahead of the curve.

**Moving forward**

Not growing and improving come at a cost. Here's a stat for you to demonstrate the point: of the original 1955 Fortune 500 list, only 12 percent of businesses existed in 2017[1]. This is referred to as the "Fortune 500 Disease," and a big reason for this is the failure to grow and improve.

The ones that are still around are the ones that adapted to changes and developments, and continued to grow and improve.

Suffice to say, it is important to grow, and improve.

Kaizen - the practice of committing to continuously and consistently grow and improve - is a big part of long-term productivity and effectiveness. If you want to stay at the top of your game in the long term, you have to work on growing and improving.

---

Kaizen is an essential principle for long-term growth and impact. But just as important as the long term is the short term, and in the next chapter, we will learn how to make the most of the short term. This is important if you want to stay at the top of your game, day in day out.

My general attitude to life is to enjoy every minute of every day. I never do anything with a feeling of, "Oh God, I've got to do this today" - Richard Branson

# Chapter 13

## Taking Care Of The Short Term

Radical productivity isn't just about the long term or the short term. You need to be able to manage both time frames effectively in order to truly unlock your productivity and potential.

In the last two chapters, we looked at how to effectively manage the long term so that you set yourself up for the most impact. In this chapter, we will explore how you can deal with things effectively in the short term.

Enter: Mindfulness.

**Mindfulness**

Mindfulness is all about being present, i.e., being focused on the present moment. It's a psychological process of bringing your attention to what is happening now, rather than getting focused on what has, or will, happen.

One of the main causes of stress is worrying about what has happened or will happen - worrying about the past or the future. Mindfulness is one of the most effective ways to deal with that.

Stress has a host of negative impact on our health and well-being, and also impacts (often quite severely) how impactful and productive you are. So when you reduce stress by practising mindfulness, you will see a big improvement in your productivity.

Here are some other benefits of note:

- In order to be really effective, focus is key, and being mindful is one of the best ways to focus.

- Mindfulness is a very effective technique for getting clarity. Mindfulness helps you to ground yourself, which is a great way to get clarity on the current state of things, and that can help you decide your next course of action. Being busy just for the sake of it is a waste of time and energy. You would be better off not doing anything as that will give you time to think and get clarity on where your time and energy would be best spent. Practising mindfulness is a really effective way of identifying situations like this.

- Mindfulness improves mental energy levels, and job satisfaction, as a 2013 American Psychological Association study[1] found.
- It is also good for solving problems and boosting creativity.

**How to practice mindfulness**

Ready to get started with mindfulness?

Then follow these steps:

1. Take a few slow, deep breaths.
2. Notice your breathing. Really notice the breath going in and out. Notice what your mind does. If it wanders, just notice the distractions, let them back and bring your focus back to your breathing.

Just practice these simple steps to get started with mindfulness.

**Easy ways to practice mindfulness**

Mindfulness isn't just about meditation, it is something you can practice anytime, and for anything. Here are five ideas for ways you can easily practice mindfulness on a day-to-day basis:

1. Observe your breathing (see above).
2. Observe what you feel (e.g., the air and/or temperature on your skin).
3. Walk mindfully.
4. Eat mindfully.
5. Listen mindfully.

These five practices should get you well on your way to practising mindfulness regularly.

**Self-Awareness**

Mindfulness is not just good for getting clarity and boosting your productivity, it is also one of the best ways to develop self-awareness.

Being self-aware is absolutely essential for personal growth and impacts everything from your happiness levels to your mental health to your ability to be effective.

Being self-aware helps you unlock your potential, and helps you grow and improve yourself in ways that are most effective for you.

Self-awareness has many benefits, and mindfulness is a great way of developing that. The more you practice being mindful, the more self-aware you will become.

Yet another (great) reason to practice mindfulness regularly.

**Moving forward**

During the hustle and bustle of our busy lives, we often tend to forget about (or lose sight of) a very important fact of life - that life is a journey. Every day, every little thing we do and every experience we have - they all matter, they all add up. So it is important to acknowledge the whole journey, rather than just some selected milestones.

What you have been through, and what you are going through now - they matter. They all make you the person you are. When you enjoy the journey (rather than just focusing on a few milestones), you put yourself in a position to make the most of all that happens, and in a milestones), you put yourself in a position to make the most of all that happens, and in a position to learn from not just the ups, but also the downs. That makes you stronger, and better, in the long term. As such, mindfulness is a great practice to adopt.

On that note, mindfulness meditation is a great habit to develop generally. There are lots of benefits to practising mindfulness (I wrote about 30 of them at LifeLabMagazine.com, check them out), and it is a great way to start your day effectively. In fact, you can incorporate mindfulness into your morning system (see Chapter 5).

This practice is also very useful any time you are stressed and/or confused. It is, in fact, one of the best ways to deal with (and reduce) stress[2].

All said it is important to understand that both the long-term and short-term time frames are essential for radically improving your productivity. You cannot make any significant progress in the future if you don't have a plan, and if you don't keep growing and improving.

But there won't be a future if you fail to effectively manage your present, and that is where mindfulness comes in handy.

Practice mindfulness - it will massively benefit your health, well-being, growth, and productivity.

*Success is the sum of small efforts, repeated day in and day out* - Robert Collier

# Recap

Here's a quick recap of what you have learned so far.

In chapter 1, you learned about the greatest productivity myth. Just understanding this alone will have a significant impact on your productivity.

In chapter 2, you learned what it takes to be truly productive. You learned the basis of radical productivity, how it is different from the current definition of productivity, and why being radically productive is the way to go if you want to have impact.

In chapter 3, you learned about the myth of starting early in the morning, and why it is not the best strategy for everyone. You also learned about Chronotypes, why they matter, and how to best design your day for most impact.

In chapter 4, you learned about the myth about multitasking, the problems with it, and what you should be doing instead.

In chapter 5, you learned about how to start your day strong, in a way that enables you to have a radically productive day, day in day out. You also learned about creating an effective system that will not just have a huge impact on your productivity and results, but also improve the quality of your life.

In chapter 6, you learned about a 20-minute strategy that will help you deal with distractions and do focused work.

In chapter 7, you learned how to effectively budget, plan and manage your time. This (along with your morning system) will help you to finally master your time.

In chapter 8, you learned how to make the most of your time and do work that has impact. You also learned how to prioritise where to spend your time and energy (and where not to), and what to do with all the things that you would like to do but don't have time for.

In chapter 9, you learned a strategy that can help you do be productive even when you are feeling lazy, and/or procrastinating.

In chapter 10, you learned about the five-minute strategy that can help you get things done, especially when you are struggling to get started, or don't have the motivation.

In chapter 11, you learned about what it takes to make real progress in the long term.

In chapter 12, you learned how to keep growing, and improving. This, along with what you learned in chapter 11, will help you to get better, stronger, and more effective over time.

In chapter 13, you learned about what is important to do in the short term, to stay at your peak and do the best work you can.

Are we on the same page?

Have you missed anything?

If you have missed something, go back and review that chapter again. Often the best way to really grasp a concept is to read it more than once.

The secret of getting ahead is getting started -
Mark Twain

# Next Steps

You have finished the book, congratulations!

Most readers do not finish reading the books they start. People have the best intentions, but life gets in the way, commitments falter, distractions come up... So the fact that you have made it this far stands you out from the crowd.

It also means you are in the best position to not just improve your productivity, but radically transform it - given, of course, that you actually did read all the chapters.

If you did not, you would miss out.

Each and every one of those chapters has the ability to massively impact your productivity, and then when you put all of them together you get a radical transformation.

I am going to assume that you are one of the few who did go through the whole book (hopefully more than once), and congratulate again on your drive, patience, and persistence.

You are in a really good position to radically transform your productivity. But only if you actually apply what you have learned in this book.

**Three frogs riddle**

Have you heard the riddle about the three frogs? It goes something like this: three frogs are sitting on a log by a pond. One of the frogs decides to jump in. How many are left?

If you answered three, then you are spot on. That one frog who decided to jump in only made the decision - he didn't actually jump in, so that leaves all three of them on the log and none in the pond.

There is a big difference between making a decision and acting on it. Until you act on your decision, the decision makes a very little real impact, if any impact at all. The point is this - it is not enough to just read this book and decide to apply what you have learned. Those are two very important steps, but nothing will change until you actually apply what you have learned in your life and do so consistently. So apply what you have learned.

Application is the final piece of the puzzle

Here is the reality - not everyone who reads a book actually does anything with what they learned. And it is a crying shame because if they did, they would have improved their lives quite a bit. I understand life happens, but real results only happen when you act.

If you do nothing, you will get nothing. So don't do that.

You are in a great position - you have already started your journey on a strong footing by finishing this book. You have learned things that can (and will) transform your productivity.

Now it is time to apply them.

Start small. Don't try to apply everything at once, as that might overwhelm you. Pick one thing to try, apply it consistently for a few days/weeks - until it becomes natural, then try another.

Patience and consistency are key.

You have the building blocks. Now go build.

*The journey of a thousand miles begins with one step - Lao Tzu*

# Closing Thoughts

It is never too late to start. Only because you have been struggling with productivity and time management so far does not mean this is how it has to be forever. You can learn, and improve, especially now that you have the tools to radically improve your productivity.

On that note, you have come a long way. You have finished the book, learned some valuable principles and strategies, and have some great tools for your productivity toolbox. But this is not the end, not by a long shot - this is, in fact, just the beginning of your journey.

You have learned some great ideas and strategies - ideas that can radically transform your productivity. But like I mentioned in the last chapter, the improvement can only happen when you apply what you have learned.

I don't want you to just take my word for their effectiveness though - I want you to try them out yourself. In fact, find ways to improve on my ideas - and share them with me.

I am constantly learning myself and I am not perfect. If I missed something, or you have any suggestions, I would be keen to hear from you (leaving a comment on my website is the best way to send me your feedback).

When I set out to write this book, I wanted to create something that will make an impact. Something that will genuinely help people. Something that will change people's perception of productivity, debunk myths and misconceptions, and teach strategies that will help people make a serious impact with their work.

Only you, my reader, can tell me how successful I have been in achieving those goals.

I am not a big believer of assuming things, but there IS something I can predict: if you apply what you learn in this book, you WILL transform your productivity.

I hope you do (apply them). The ball, now, is in your court now…

Here's to you radically improving your productivity.

All the best!

Salek
31st July 2019 London, UK

**If this book has been helpful...**

The main reason for writing this book is to help as many people as possible. So it is always good to hear from anyone who has found this useful.

On that note, if you found the information in this book valuable, please consider leaving a review - reviews help the book reach other readers who can benefit from it.

Also, please spread the word - if you know anyone who this book can help, do let them know. The more people it can reach, the more it can help.

Pay it forward!

**Also by the author**

The Business Launch Code: A Step By Step Guide To Starting Your Own Business

Business Edge: 25 Tools and Strategies to Give Your Business an Edge

# About The Author

M Salek is a Peak performance and business strategist, and the founder and CEO of PeakMx (peakmx.com), a peak performance training and consultancy firm dedicated to helping individuals and businesses unlock their potential.

Salek is an avid reader, traveller, and foodie. Driven by his curiosity and passion for learning and helping others, he sits at the board of multiple non-profit organisations, and spends the bulk of his time helping people improve their lives.

To learn more, check out:
- Personal - mhasalek.com
- Work - peakmx.com
- Twitter - twitter.com/mhasalek

# References

*Introduction*

1. Bls.gov. (2019). Productivity and Costs, First Quarter 2019, Revised. [online] https://www.bls.gov/news.release/prod2.nr0.htm

2. Stress in America: Paying with our Health. (2015). American Psychological Association. http://www.apa.org/news/press/releases/stress/2014/stress-report.pdf

*Chapter 2*

1. Leveson, I. (1967). Reductions in Hours of Work as a Source of Productivity Growth. Journal of Political Economy, [online] 75(2), pp.199-204. https://www.journals.uchicago.edu/doi/pdfplus/10.1086/259266

2. Ericsson, Karl & Krampe, Ralf & Tesch-Roemer, Clemens. (1993). The Role of Deliberate Practice in the Acquisition of Expert Performance. Psychological Review. 100. 363-406. 10.1037//0033-295X.100.3.363.

3. The Productivity of Working Hours, The Economic Journal, Volume 125, Issue 589, 1 December 2015, Pages 2052–2076, https://doi.org/10.1111/ecoj.12166

4. Spurgeon A, Harrington JM, Cooper CL Health and safety problems associated with long working hours: a review of the current position. Occupational and Environmental Medicine 1997;54:367-375

*Chapter 3*

1. How Much Sleep Do We Really Need? National Sleep Foundation, www.sleepfoundation.org/excessive-sleepiness/support/how-much-sleep-do-we- really-need.

2. Göran Kecklund, Torbjörn Åkerstedt, Arne Lowden, Morning Work: Effects of Early Rising on Sleep and Alertness, Sleep, Volume 20, Issue 3, March 1997, Pages 215–223, https://doi.org/10.1093/sleep/20.3.215

3. Clodoré, M., Benoit, O., Foret, J. et al. Europ. J. Appl. Physiol. (1987) 56: 403. https://doi.org/10.1007/BF00417767

4. Vohs, K. D., Baumeister, R. F., Schmeichel, B. J., Twenge, J. M., Nelson, N. M., & Tice, D. M. (2014). Making choices impairs subsequent self-control: A limited-resource account of decision making, self-regulation, and active initiative. Motivation Science, 1(S), 19-42. http://dx.doi.org10.1037/2333-8113.1.S.19

5. Boatman, T. (2018). *8 Eye-Opening Employee Productivity Statistics*. [online] Qnnect.com. https://www.qnnect.com/blog/8-eye-opening-employee-productivity- statistics

6. Grandviewresearch.com. (2019). *Personalized Medicine Market Size & Forecast | Industry Report, 2025*. [online] https://www.grandviewresearch.com/industry- analysis/personalized-medicine-market

7. Schein, V. E., Maurer, E. H., & Novak, J. F. (1977). Impact of flexible working hours on productivity. *Journal of Applied Psychology*, 62(4), 463-465. http://dx.doi.org/10.1037/0021-9010.62.4.463

Chapter 4

1. Aalto University. "Movie research results: Multitasking overloads the brain: The brain works most efficiently when it can focus on a single task for a longer period of time." ScienceDaily. ScienceDaily, 25 April 2017. www.sciencedaily.com/releases/2017/04/170425092429.htm

2. Juha M. Lahnakoski, Iiro P. Jääskeläinen, Mikko Sams, Lauri Nummenmaa. Neural mechanisms for integrating consecutive and interleaved natural events. *Human Brain Mapping*, 2017; DOI: 10.1002/hbm.23591

3. *Multitasking: Switching Costs*. https://www.apa.org, 2006, https://www.apa.org/research/action/multitask.

Chapter 5

1. Vohs, K. D., Baumeister, R. F., Schmeichel, B. J., Twenge, J. M., Nelson, N. M., & Tice, D. M. (2014). Making choices impairs subsequent self-control: A limited- resource account of decision making, self-regulation, and active initiative. *Motivation Science*, 1(S), 19-42. http://dx.doi.org/10.1037/2333-8113.1.S.19

2. *What You Need to Know about Willpower: The Psychological Science of Self-Control* (2012). [online] https://www.apa.org/helpcenter/willpower

3. Ludwig, F. (1997). How routine facilitates wellbeing in older women. *Occupational Therapy International*, [online] 4(3), pp.215-230. https://onlinelibrary.wiley.com/doi/abs/10.1002/oti.57

4. Ben-zur, H. and Zeidner, M. (1995). Coping patterns and affective reactions under community crisis and daily routine conditions. *Anxiety, Stress & Coping*, [online] 8(3), pp.185-201. https://www.tandfonline.com/doi/abs/10.1080/10615809508249372

Chapter 6

1. Talent Works International. (2018). 10 workplace stats you don't want to miss - infographic - Talent Works International. [online] https://www.talent-works.com/2018/08/22/workplace-stats-infographic/

2. Frequent Short Rest Breaks from Computer Work: Effects on Productivity and Well-Being at Two Field Sites. Taylor & Francis, www.tandfonline.com/doi/abs/10.1080/001401397188396

3. TAYLOR, W. (2005). Transforming Work Breaks to Promote Health. American Journal of Preventive Medicine, [online] 29(5), pp.461-465. https://www.sciencedirect.com/science/article/abs/pii/S0749379705003454

4. ScienceDaily. (2018). Changes in stress after meditation. [online] https://www.sciencedaily.com/releases/2018/06/180621111955.htm

5. Harvard Health Publishing. The Importance of Stretching. Harvard Health, www.health.harvard.edu/staying-healthy/the-importance-of-stretching

6. Pathak, Neha. (2017). Why Sitting Too Much Is Bad for Your Health. [PowerPoint presentation]. https://www.webmd.com/fitness-exercise/ss/slideshow-sitting-health

7. Capaldi C, Dopko RL, Zelenski J. The relationship between nature connectedness and happiness: a meta-analysis. Frontiers in Psychology. 2014. doi:10.3389/fpsyg.2014.00976

8. ScienceDaily. (2019). Just 20 minutes of contact with nature will lower stress hormone levels, reveals new study. [online] https://www.sciencedaily.com/releases/2019/04/190404074915.htm

9. Pearson DG, Craig T. The great outdoors? Exploring the mental health benefits of natural environments. Frontiers in Psychology. 2014;5:1178. doi: 10.3389/fpsyg.2014.01178 + Bratman GN, Hamilton JP, Hahn KS, et al. Nature experience reduces rumination and subgenual prefrontal cortex activation.

10. Proceedings of the National Academy of Sciences of the United States of America. 2015(112);28:8567-8572. doi: 10.1073/pnas.1510459112

11. Oppezzo, M. and Schwartz, D. (2014). Give Your Ideas Some Legs: The Positive Effect of Walking on Creative Thinking. [ebook] Journal of Experimental Psychology: Learning, Memory and Cognition. https://www.apa.org/pubs/journals/releases/xlm-a0036577.pdf

12. Coulson, J., McKenna, J. and Field, M. (2008), "Exercising at work and self reported work performance", International Journal of Workplace Health

Management, Vol. 1 No. 3, pp. 176-197. https://doi.org/10.1108/17538350810926534

## Chapter 7

1. Stillman, J. (2018). *Elon Musk and Bill Gates Schedule Their Days in 5-Minute Chunks.* [online] Curiosity.com. https://curiosity.com/topics/elon-musk-and-bill-gates-schedule-their-days-in-5-minute-chunks-curiosity/.

2. Cornerstoneondemand.com. (2014). *New Research Reveals Biggest Productivity Killers for America's Workforce.* [online] https://www.cornerstoneondemand.com/company/news/press-releases/new-research-reveals-biggest-productivity-killers-america%E2%80%99s-workforce

3. MULLER, G. (2009). SYSTEM AND CONTEXT MODELING — THE ROLE OF TIME-BOXING AND MULTI-VIEW ITERATION. *Systems Research Forum*, [online] 03(02), pp.139-152. https://www.worldscientific.com/doi/abs/10.1142/S1793966609000092

## Chapter 8

1. Gallup, I. (2015). *Employees Who Use Their Strengths Outperform Those Who Don't.* [online] https://www.gallup.com/workplace/236561/employees-strengths-outperform-don.aspx

2. *Consumer Email Is on the Decline - but Almost Everything Else 'Email' Is on the Rise.* Attentiv, 26 Jan. 2016, attentiv.com/email-takes-time

3. Kostadin Kushlev, Elizabeth W.Dunn (2014) "Checking email less frequently reduces stress" Computers in Human Behavior Volume 43, February 2015, Pages 220-228 [online] https://www.sciencedirect.com/science/article/pii/S0747563214005810

## Chapter 10

1. Gaille, B. (2017). *19 Lazy Procrastination Statistics.* [online] BrandonGaille.com. https://brandongaille.com/17-lazy-procrastination-statistics/

2. Radwan, M. (n.d.). *Why procrastination causes stress | 2KnowMySelf.* [online] 2knowmyself.com. https://www.2knowmyself.com/Why_procrastination_causes_stress

3. Thompson, D. (2014). *The Procrastination Doom Loop—and How to Break It.* [online] The Atlantic. https://www.theatlantic.com/business/archive/2014/08/the-procrastination-loop-and-how-to-break-it/379142

4. Senécal, C., Koestner, R. and Vallerand, R. (1995). Self-Regulation and Academic Procrastination. *The Journal of Social Psychology*, [online] 135(5),

pp.607-619. https://www.tandfonline.com/doi/abs/10.1080/00224545.1995.9712234

5. Zarick, L. and Stonebraker, R. (2009). I'll do it Tomorrow: The Logic of Procrastination. College Teaching, [online] 57(4), pp.211-215. https://www.tandfonline.com/doi/abs/10.1080/87567550903218687

6. Steel, P. (2007). The nature of procrastination: A meta-analytic and theoretical review of quintessential self-regulatory failure. Psychological Bulletin, [online] 133(1), pp.65-94. https://psycnet.apa.org/record/2006-23058-004?doi=1

Chapter 11

1. Amabile, T. and Kramer, S. (2011). The Power of Small Wins. [online] Harvard Business Review. https://hbr.org/2011/05/the-power-of-small-wins

2. Kullberg, A., Runesson, U., Marton, F., Vikström, A., Nilsson, P., Mårtensson, P. and Häggström, J. (2016). Teaching one thing at a time or several things together? – teachers changing their way of handling the object of learning by being engaged in a theory-based professional learning community in mathematics and science. Teachers and Teaching, [online] 22(6), pp.745-759. Available at:https://www.tandfonline.com/doi/abs/10.1080/13540602.2016.1158957

Chapter 12

1. Perry, M. (2017). Fortune 500 firms 1955 v. 2017: Only 60 remain, thanks to the creative destruction that fuels economic prosperity. [online] http://www.aei.org. Available at: http://www.aei.org/publication/fortune-500-firms-1955-v-2017-only-12-remain-thanks-to-the-creative-destruction-that-fuels-economic-prosperity

Chapter 13

1. Hülsheger, U., Alberts, H., Feinholdt, A. and Lang, J. (2013). Benefits of mindfulness at work: The role of mindfulness in emotion regulation, emotional exhaustion, and job satisfaction. Journal of Applied Psychology, [online] 98(2), pp.310-325. https://psycnet.apa.org/record/2012-34922-001?doi=1

2. Janssen, Math, et al. "Effects of Mindfulness-Based Stress Reduction on Employees' Mental Health: A Systematic Review." PLOS ONE, Public Library of Science, journals.plos.org/plosone/article?id=10.1371%2Fjournal.pone.0191332

Miscellaneous

1. Bryson, A. and Forth, J. (2007). Are There Day of the Week Productivity Effects?. [online] Cep.lse.ac.uk. http://cep.lse.ac.uk/pubs/download/mhrldp0004.pdf

2. Fritz, C., Ellis, A., Demsey, C., Lin, B. and Guros, F. (2013). Embracing work breaks: Recovering from work stress. [online] Thriving.berkeley.edu. http://thriving.berkeley.edu/sites/default/files/Embracing%20Work%20Breaks%20(Eschleman%20Lecture).pdf

3. Rekik, M., Cordeau, J. and Soumis, F. (2009). Implicit shift scheduling with multiple breaks and work stretch duration restrictions. Journal of Scheduling, [online] 13(1), pp.49-75. https://link.springer.com/article/10.1007/s10951-009-0114-z

4. Oh, J. and Tajik, J. (2003). The return of cardiac time intervals. [online] http://www.onlinejacc.org. http://www.onlinejacc.org/content/42/8/1471.abstract
5.Nelson, Richard R. "Research on Productivity Growth and Productivity Differences: Dead Ends and New Departures." Journal of Economic Literature, vol. 19, no. 3, 1981, pp. 1029–1064. JSTOR, www.jstor.org/stable/2724327

5. Kirchhoff, J. and Kirchhoff, B. (2019). Family Contributions to Productivity and Profitability in Small Business. [online] Questia.com. https://www.questia.com/library/journal/1G1-6164805/family-contributions-to-productivity-and-profitability

6. Rogers, A., Hwang, W. and Scott, L. (2004). The Effects of Work Breaks on Staff Nurse Performance. JONA: The Journal of Nursing Administration, [online] 34(11), pp.512-519. https://journals.lww.com/jonajournal/fulltext/2004/11000/the_effects_of_work_bre aks_on_staff_nurse.7.aspx

7. Perron, P. and Zhu, X. (2005). Structural breaks with deterministic and stochastic trends. Journal of Econometrics, [online] 129(1-2), pp.65-119. https://www.sciencedirect.com/science/article/pii/S0304407604001666

8. Eduardo Miranda. 2011. Time boxing planning: buffered moscow rules. SIGSOFT Softw. Eng. Notes 36, 6 (November 2011), 1-5. DOI=http://dx.doi.org/10.1145/2047414.2047428

9. MULLER, G. (2009). SYSTEM AND CONTEXT MODELING — THE ROLE OF TIME-BOXING AND MULTI-VIEW ITERATION. Systems Research Forum, [online] 03(02), pp.139-152. https://www.worldscientific.com/doi/abs/10.1142/S1793966609000092

10. Wilson, R. (1994), "An Improved Goal-oriented Method for Measuring Productivity", International Journal of Operations & Production Management, Vol. 14 No. 1, pp. 50-59. https://doi.org/10.1108/01443579410049306

11. Valmohammadi, Changiz. (2010). Identification and prioritization of critical success factors of knowledge management in Iranian SMEs: An experts' view. African Journal of Business Management. 4. 915-924

12. Slack, N. (1994), "The Importance Performance Matrix as a Determinant of Improvement Priority", International Journal of Operations & Production Management, Vol. 14 No. 5, pp. 59-75. https://doi.org/10.1108/01443579410056803

13. Prioritising Effectively. The Open www.open.ac.uk/choose/unison/develop/my-skills/prioritising-effectively.

14. Hollis, Ashley-Tate, "Cures for Procrastination in College Students" (2012). A with Honors Projects. http://spark.parkland.edu/ah/68

15. Procrastination and Personality, Performance, and Mood. Personality and Individual Differences, Pergamon, 16 Nov. 2000, www.sciencedirect.com/science/article/pii/S0191886900000131

16. Work Performance: Is It One Thing or Many Things? The Multidimensionality of Performance in a Middle Eastern Context. Taylor & Francis, www.tandfonline.com/doi/abs/10.1080/713769689

17. Journal of Online Learning Research Volume 2, Number 3, Dec 20, 2016 ISSN 2374-1473 Publisher: Association for the Advancement of Computing in Education (AACE), Waynesville, NC USA

18. Boatman, Tony. "8 Eye-Opening Employee Productivity Statistics." Qnnect, www.qnnect.com/blog/8-eye-opening-employee-productivity-statistics.

19. Chua, Celestine. "11 Simple Tips to Effective Email Management." Lifehack, Lifehack, 9 May 2014, www.lifehack.org/articles/productivity/11-simple-tips-effective-email-management.html

20. McKenzie, Jessica. "Good Company." APA Center for Organizational Excellence, www.apaexcellence.org/resources/goodcompany/blog/2012/03/exercising-at- work-boosts-prod.php

21. Stress in the Workplace: Meeting the Challenge. Health Advocate. http://healthadvocate.com/downloads/webinars/stress-workplace.pdf

22. Ericsson, K. A. (2014). Creative genius: A view from the expert-performance approach. In D. K. Simonton (Ed.), The Wiley-Blackwell handbook of genius (pp. 321-349). New York: Wiley

23. *Ward, P., Ericsson, K. A., & Williams, & A. M. (2013). Complex perceptual-cognitive expertise in a simulated task environment. Journal of Cognitive Engineering and Decision Making, 7, 231-254*

24. *Duckworth, A. L., Kirby, T., Tsukayama, E., Berstein, K., & Ericsson, K. A. (2011). Deliberate practice spells success: Why grittier competitors triumph at the National Spelling Bee. Social Psychological and Personality Science, 2, 174-181*

25. *Ericsson, K. A., Nandagopal, K., & Roring, R. W. (2009). An expert-performance approach to the study of giftedness. In L. Shavinina (Ed.), International handbook of giftedness (pp. 129-153). Berlin, Germany: Springer Science + Business Media*

26. *2016 U.S. Cross-Platform Future in Focus. Comscore, Inc., www.comscore.com/Insights/Presentations-and-Whitepapers/2016/2016-US-Cross-Platform-Future-in-Focus*

27. *Journaling for Mental Health - Health Encyclopedia - University of Rochester Medical Center. [online] https://www.urmc.rochester.edu/encyclopedia/content.aspx?ContentID=4552&Co ntentTypeID=1*

Author's note: This list is not exhaustive - some of the researches reviewed weren't necessarily relevant, and as such were not referenced. Some though, I just forgot to include in my list. But all the important researches and references - the ones that have had a direct impact on my research for this book - are included in the list above.

**NOTES:**